This book belongs to

_____

This book is dedicated to parents, educators, and counselors everywhere. We have the most important job nurturing the next generation.

"Everything will be fine, Mom," I said as I
offered my mother a gentle reminder.

I'm able to stay calm even in the most worrisome situations.

When I accidentally kicked the ball out of bounds instead of in the goal, I would simply say...

If my new shoes were too big, I would think...

If I was picked last, I would exclaim...

I haven't always been so worry free.

Once upon a time, I really could be quite worrisome.

When I was on a boat with my family, negative thoughts would fill my head...

Until one day, my friend, Zen Ninja, suggested that I try a fun way to change my thinking.

WORRY WHEEL

What if...?
What if...

My handwriting isn't very good

What if people laugh at me?

hA hA

I worry that people will laugh at my hair

What will people think?

I worry because I can't kick a ball straight

common worries

I worry that people will say my shoes are scruffy.

I worry that other people think I am not very clever

Things I CAN'T CONTROL

How much free time I have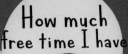

The weather

Taking classes online or going to in person school

What others say or think

Not being invited to the party

Things I CAN CONTROL

sleeping well to stay strong and healthy

Washing my hands

Telling others my feelings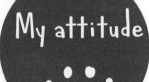

My attitude

Being kind

CIRCLE of CONTROL

So I tried it.

I stopped the worry wheel from rolling in my head.

Determined that it was not something I could control.

And took a deep breath in.

Then, I blew the worry away.

And do you know what happened next?

It worked!

From that day on, I felt a lot less worrisome and a whole lot calmer.

Using this circle of control and dandelion strategy could be your secret weapon against worrisome thoughts.

Visit us at NinjaLifeHacks.tv to let go of your worries
with our Ninja Life Hacks journal.

@marynhin   @GrowGrit
#NinjaLifeHacks

Mary Nhin   Ninja Life Hacks

Ninja Life Hacks

Printed in Great Britain
by Amazon

24409743R00021